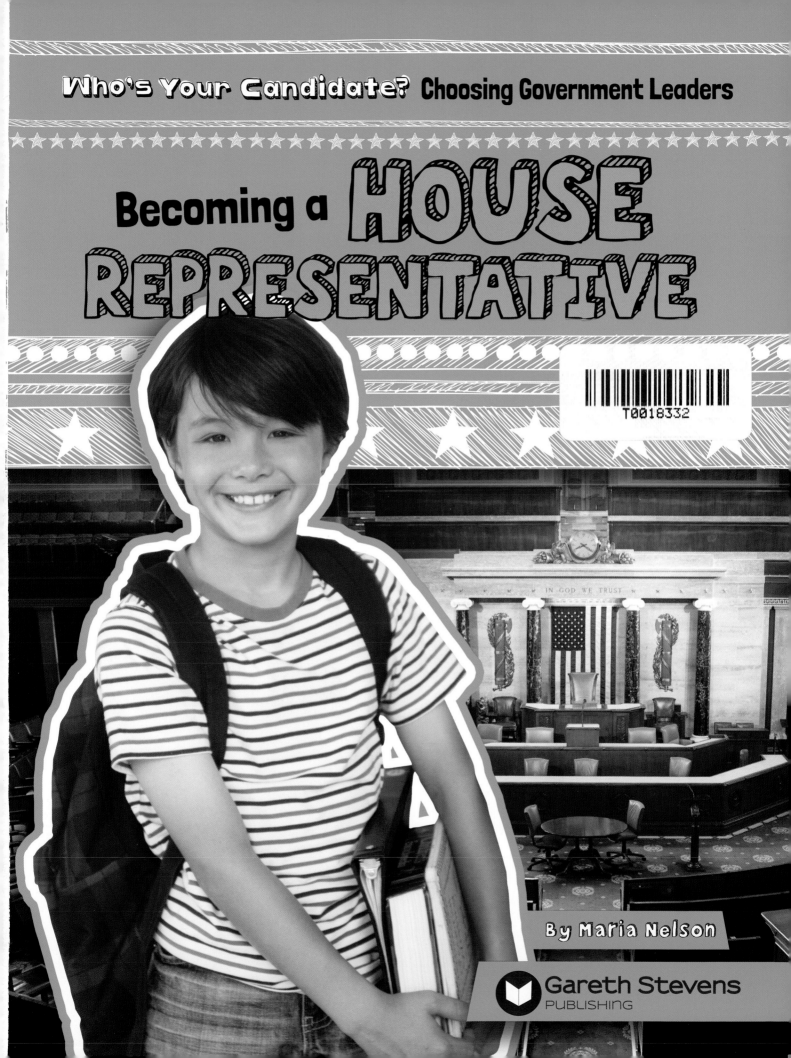

Becoming a HOUSE REPRESENTATIVE

T0018332

By Maria Nelson

Gareth Stevens
PUBLISHING

Please visit our website, www.garethstevens.com. For a free color catalog of all our high-quality books, call toll free 1-800-542-2595 or fax 1-877-542-2596.

Cataloging-in-Publication Data

Nelson, Maria.
Becoming a house representative / by Maria Nelson.
p. cm. — (Who's your candidate? Choosing government leaders)
Includes index.
ISBN 978-1-4824-4035-5 (pbk.)
ISBN 978-1-4824-4036-2 (6-pack)
ISBN 978-1-4824-4037-9 (library binding)
1. United States. — Congress. — House — Juvenile literature. 2. Legislators — United States — Juvenile literature. I. Nelson, Maria. II. Title.
JK1319.N45 2016
328.73'072—d23

Published in 2016 by
Gareth Stevens Publishing
111 East 14th Street, Suite 349
New York, NY 10003

Copyright © 2016 Gareth Stevens Publishing

Designer: Andrea Davison-Bartolotta
Editor: Kristen Nelson

Photo credits: Cover, p. 1 (main) Sri Maiava Rusden/Getty Images; cover, p. 1 (background) Brendan Hoffman/Getty Images; p. 4 Vlad G/Shutterstock.com; p. 5 Dirk Anschutz/Getty Images; p. 7 Gabriella Demczuk/Getty Images; pp. 8–9 Bill O'Leary/The Washington Post/Getty Images; p. 10 Monkey Business Images/Shutterstock.com; p. 11 Bill Clark/CQ Roll Call/Getty Images; p. 12 Steve Debenport/Getty Images; p. 13 Hill Street Studios/Eric Raptosh/Getty Images; p. 15 Kathryn Scott Osler/Getty Images; p. 16 Ariel Skelley/Getty Images; pp. 17, 24–25 Mark Wilson/Getty Images; p. 19 Jupiterimages/Photos.com/Thinkstock; p. 21 Fuse/Thinkstock; pp. 22–23 Alex Wong/Getty Images; p. 27 Brendan Smialowski/AFP/Getty Images; p. 29 89studio/Shutterstock.com.

Printed in the United States of America

CPSIA compliance information: Batch #CW16GS: For further information contact Gareth Stevens, New York, New York at 1-800-542-2595.

CONTENTS

Words in the glossary appear in **bold** type the first time they are used in the text.

Represent!

What would you do if your school was getting rid of your favorite activity? Maybe you love playing in the band and you find out that there won't be a band next year. Or perhaps there's something about your community you think needs to change. You don't have to sit back and accept your world as it is. You can have a say!

You can be elected to be a representative in your class's or school's student government group or serve as a leader in a club. Working toward one of these positions is much like becoming a member of the US House of Representatives!

In the House

A representative in the House is a member of Congress, the main lawmaking body in the United States. There are 435 members in the House from all 50 US states. The number of representatives from each state is based on that state's population. Montana only has one representative, but New York State has 27! Each represents a district, or small part of the state.

US Capitol

The word "representative" means "someone who stands for something." Both young people and House representatives often run for an office because they have something in particular they want to stand for.

House Basics

The House of Representatives makes up half of the **legislative** branch of the US government. The other half is the Senate. These two houses of Congress are both made up of the citizens who live in a state and are elected to their positions.

The US government is based on a system of checks and balances. Congress makes sure the executive branch of government—headed by the president—doesn't have too much power. But the president can **veto** laws made by Congress. The highest court in the United States, the Supreme Court, makes sure Congress and the president follow the laws set up in the Constitution.

Your Turn!

As a student leader, you're also part of a system of checks and balances. You may represent the opinions of your classmates to the Parent Teacher Association, the principal, or the school board. You represent the needs of students to adults who might not know students care about something, such as a new dress code or school lunch **policy**.

A big part of being in Congress or a leader in your school or community is working well with others. If you're good at finding **compromises**, positions like these might be a good fit for you!

The House of Representatives and Senate serve to check and balance each other, too. Major bills are proposed in the House first, as the House is supposed to show the will of the people. But the Senate takes a longer time to **debate** bills, allowing consideration of long-term effects.

Representatives' close connection to their districts balances senators' more distant position of representing a whole state.

The US Constitution created differences between the two to support the government's checks and balances.

	House of Representatives	Senate
age	must be 25 or older	must be 30 or older
length of citizenship	at least 7 years	at least 9 years
length of term	2 years	6 years
number of members	435	100
number of reps from each state	depends on population	2

Short-Term Job

Members of the House of Representatives only serve 2-year terms because they're supposed to be the voice of the people. The Founding Fathers believed keeping the term short would make it more likely that US citizens' needs would be represented. They wanted House representatives to have close connections with their **constituency**.

Who Can Run?

Once the base qualifications are met for the House of Representatives, anyone can run! California congressman Michael Honda, for example, started his career as a teacher and school principal. Massachusetts congresswoman Katherine Clark was a lawyer for many years before entering politics.

Experience in politics isn't necessary for someone running for a seat in the House. In fact, people often run for the position in order to make changes to the area they live in. Like you, they might start out as leaders in community groups working for better road conditions or more parks.

Your Turn!

Just like Congress, your school might have qualifications for those running for student leadership positions. Be sure your grades are good enough and complete forms, essays, or **petitions** you need in order to run. In addition, talk to the teachers and other students in the group. Make sure you run for a position you would be good at and enjoy!

House representatives can be men or women and be of any background. Mia Love, a representative from Utah shown here, was the first black Republican woman elected to Congress in 2012.

Having some political experience often makes becoming a House representative easier, though. Many representatives start out as representatives or senators in their home cities or states. Many state legislators also represent a smaller area within their state and will already know how to work with their constituency. State positions also make politicians' names more familiar to those they represent. People are more likely to vote for someone they've heard of when it's federal election time!

Before announcing that they're running, many candidates "test the waters" of their district. They make phone calls and travel around to see if they have a good chance to be elected.

Your Turn!

Think about the leadership position you want. When working to get elected, highlight the experience you've had that will make you good at the job! Will you need to do a lot of public speaking? Talk about your time on the debate team. Are there big events to plan? Remind everyone of your work planning the school dance.

Doing volunteer work is a great way to try a lot of things and be in leadership roles. You can build up experiences to run for a student council position in the future. Politicians do this, too!

The Campaign

Once someone has decided to run for a seat in the House, the campaign begins! Candidates often need to spend a lot of money to set up events to meet constituents, travel, and make signs, buttons, and T-shirts. Fundraising can be really hard, and sometimes an inability to raise enough money will stop a campaign before it starts.

Once a candidate has raised or spent $5,000 for the campaign, he or she has to register with the Federal Election Commission. There are many rules about campaign fundraising that those running for Congress need to know and follow.

The constituency

Potential House representatives need to know a lot about their constituency. Who lives in a congressperson's district often decides what kinds of policies they'll support. Representatives from a very poor district may work for a higher **minimum wage**. Those from a rural district might fight for laws protecting farmers' rights.

It's important for those running for a seat in the House to spend time in their district, getting to know the people they'll be representing.

One major part of a successful House representative campaign is advertising. Many candidates make TV commercials that air in the weeks leading up to the election. They may write **editorials** or put ads in the local newspaper.

Many candidates are using social media to connect directly with their constituents. Facebook, Twitter, and YouTube allow candidates to spread their message in a more personal, casual way. Often, candidates have a staff member working specifically on social media advertising. Michigan representative Justin Amash has said that he's the only person who writes to constituents on his Facebook page, though!

Young Voters Spread the Word

Connecting to constituents on the Internet is a key part of campaigning now. The main reason for this is reaching younger voters who don't watch local news stations or read the newspaper. In addition, social media allows voters to share a candidate's message without the campaign team having to do more work!

Because the term limit is so short, some longtime representatives might feel like they're constantly campaigning. John Dingell Jr. holds the record for longest-serving representative with more than 59 years!

Your Campaign!

There are many similarities between campaigning for the House of Representatives and campaigning for a student leadership position. Like a congressional candidate, you need to get your name out there. When running for a school-wide election, such as student council, you'll need to attend as many school events as you can. Meeting a wide variety of your fellow students will help you once you announce your candidacy.

Looking to be a class or club officer requires a similar approach. Let your club and classmates know you care about being part of the group by supporting events, fundraisers, and others' activities.

Political Parties

Many congressional candidates run as a member of one of the two main political parties, the Democrats and the Republicans. They can also run without a party or as a third-party candidate—or a member of one of the many smaller political parties—such as the Green Party.

Also like candidates for the House, you should advertise your campaign! Posters hung around the school are a great way to do this.

Getting your name out to voters is just the first step of your campaign. The next step is to spread your message, or platform. Your platform might be based on your reason for running for a position. Maybe you're unhappy with the field trips chosen for the Art Club last year and you'd like to plan different ones. Or perhaps you think your class should do a talent show for a fundraiser rather than selling wrapping paper.

Your platform can include promising certain changes. However, be sure the changes you promise are actually things you can do. Talk to a parent or teacher about your plans just in case.

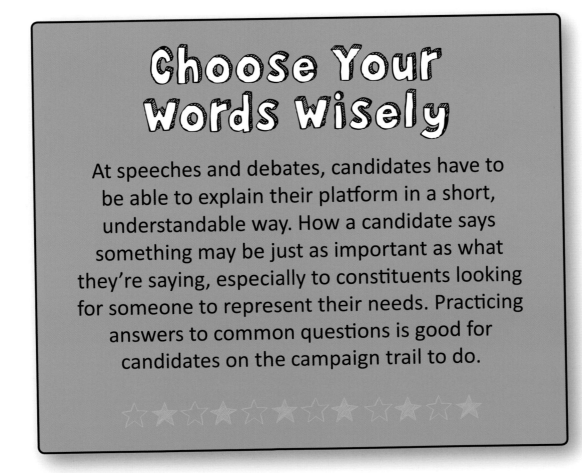

Choose Your Words Wisely

At speeches and debates, candidates have to be able to explain their platform in a short, understandable way. How a candidate says something may be just as important as what they're saying, especially to constituents looking for someone to represent their needs. Practicing answers to common questions is good for candidates on the campaign trail to do.

Whether you're running for a student council position or trying to lead a club or organization, it's important to know your platform well and be able to answer questions about it.

Time to Vote

Elections for the House of Representatives occur every 2 years in November. The US Constitution states that the election for House representatives should be based on popular vote, meaning every person's vote is counted toward a total. This is another way the Founding Fathers tried to make it the "people's house."

Every time an election occurs, a whole new House is created. Any bills or issues that were part of the previous House are gone. Since **incumbents** win many seats, this can be frustrating. It allows for new representatives to make their mark on Congress, though!

Sometimes a representative dies in office or steps down before the term is up. A member of the House can only be replaced by a special election. That's how former representative of Hawaii Charles Djou was elected in 2010.

Primary

If more than one candidate in a political party is running for an open seat in the House, the state will hold a primary election first. States hold different kinds of primaries, but one common kind lets the people registered to vote in a party choose who will run from that party.

Getting the Job Done

Much of House representatives' time is spent in Washington, DC, making laws. Each representative is on two House committees, such as foreign affairs, armed services, or the budget. Most representatives are part of committees they're interested in or have knowledge about already.

Your Turn!

What you'll do after winning your election depends on the position! Student council members often have to attend meetings, plan events, and debate topics that come up in the school. Student leaders often represent their team or club to the student council, encourage other members, and come up with ways to make money or have fun!

A House representative spends a lot of time researching how proposed bills will affect their district. He or she spends as much time as possible in their home district, too. Groups and citizens from that district can contact their representative to raise concerns, ask for money to fix bridges and roads, and show support or dislike for government policies.

Members of House committees have to consider the different sides of issues, such how much money a new government program should receive.

STAFF D

MR. ROGERS
CHAIRMAN

MR. DIAZ-BALART

MR. FRELINGHUYSEN

MR. ADERHOLT

RODNEY

25

After the Election

On the first day of a new Congress, new House representatives take an **oath** of office. In it, they promise to support the Constitution, be faithful to the United States, and do their duties the best they can.

The Speaker of the House is also elected at the beginning of a new Congress. Members of each party **nominate** someone, and every representative votes. The person who receives the majority of the votes wins the position. A House Majority Leader and Minority Leader are also chosen, but this happens before Congress begins. Representatives who have already served several terms commonly hold these leadership positions.

Your Turn!

Once elected to your position, look back at your platform. What did you promise those in your class or club? What are the first steps you can take to fulfill these promises? Make sure to ask those in the group to help! It's hard to make big changes on your own, and you will start to build a strong community—led by you!

The Speaker of the House has more duties than a regular representative. Usually a leader in the majority party, the Speaker can decide when bills are debated and voted on.

John Boehner

You—in Congress!

Representatives are able to run at age 25—that's not all that far away for an eager future politician! Until then, there are many things you can do to prepare to run for the House of Representatives. First, pay attention in school, especially in history and social studies classes. It's important to know the basics of the US Constitution since that's what the House and other government bodies are based on. Practice public speaking every chance you get, too. Doing plays or the debate team can help you do this well.

Of course, working as a student leader can get you great experience for a future in politics!

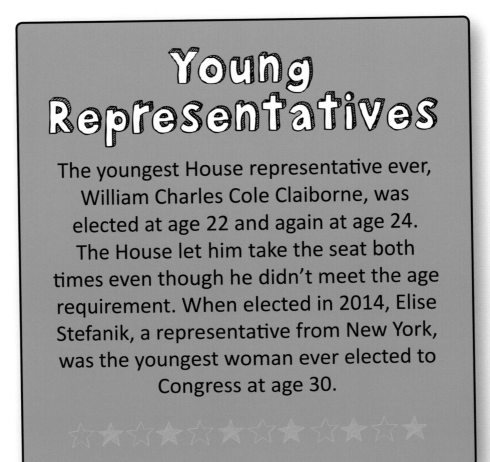

Young Representatives

The youngest House representative ever, William Charles Cole Claiborne, was elected at age 22 and again at age 24. The House let him take the seat both times even though he didn't meet the age requirement. When elected in 2014, Elise Stefanik, a representative from New York, was the youngest woman ever elected to Congress at age 30.

Building Your Résumé

• **Volunteer!** Take part in community clothing drives, serve at a soup kitchen, or give time to groups like Habitat for Humanity that help those in need.

• **Get involved!** Join clubs and organizations in school and in the community that interest you. It's even better if they help you with skills you could use in politics such as public speaking, writing, and working with others.

• **Stay connected!** If you're close with a teacher or group leader, keep in touch with them even after you've left the class or group. Knowing a lot of people in your community is important for a House representative.

• **Stay in school!** Education is very important for House representatives. Keep your grades up and aim for at least a college degree, as most representatives have them.

• **Reach out!** Most representatives can be reached by e-mail or on social media. Ask questions or even volunteer to work on campaigns.

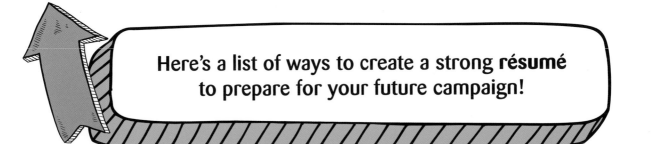

Here's a list of ways to create a strong **résumé** to prepare for your future campaign!

GLOSSARY

compromise: a way of two sides reaching agreement in which each gives up something to end an argument

constituency: the people who live and vote in an area

debate: to argue a side. Also, an argument or public discussion.

editorial: a piece of writing that gives an opinion

incumbent: a person who holds an office or position presently

legislative: having to do with making laws

minimum wage: the lowest amount of money a person can be paid per hour of work

nominate: to formally choose someone as a candidate

oath: a formal promise

petition: a written request signed by many people asking for an action to be taken

policy: a plan of general and future decisions and positions

résumé: a list of accomplishments often given when applying for a job

veto: using the power of the US president to not allow a new law or policy

FOR MORE INFORMATION

BOOKS

Cooper, Ilene. *A Woman in the House and Senate: How Women Came to the United States Congress, Broke Down Barriers, and Changed the Country.* New York, NY: Abrams Books for Young Readers, 2014.

Krieg, Katherine. *Congress.* Vero Beach, FL: Rourke Educational Media, 2015.

Spath, Carolyn E. W. *Standing in the Shoes of a Member of the House of Representatives.* New York, NY: Cavendish Square Publishing, 2016.

WEBSITES

House of Representatives
www.congressforkids.net/Legislativebranch_house.htm
Read a great summary of what the House of Representatives does and how someone can be elected to it.

How to Run for Student Council
homeworktips.about.com/od/makingthegrades/a/studentcouncil.htm
Would you like to have a say at your school? Use this guide to learn more about being involved with student council!

INDEX